This book is dedicated to my parents, siblings, wife, and children

Acknowledgment

I am grateful to my students for volunteering to proofread the numerous drafts, special mention to Manya Gulia, Aaron Martins, and Nicholas Hatzis, who spent countless hours reviewing in the most reliable and timely manner.

Table of Contents

Chapter 1 Gold Standard and US Dollar as a Reserve Currency

The Gold Standard and the US dollar as the reserve currency

We look at the history and background of the currency market so that we have a good perspective of how things were and how the global financial markets might change in the future. We all live in a world where the US dollar is the major reserve currency, but this has not always been the case. Before we had the US dollar, we had the Pound Sterling as the reserve currency and even before that, we had the French Franc. If you are interested in this, you should read how the history of a reserve currency is related to the rise and fall of empires. However, in this chapter, we will look at the modern history of currency related to the US dollar and the gold standard after 1860.

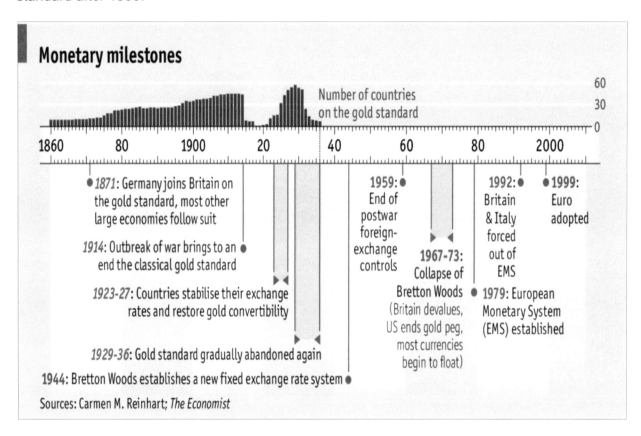

In 1871, Germany along with the other major economies joined Britain on the gold standard. In the chart above, you can see that the number of countries on the gold standard rose sharply in the 20th century before the numbers fell.

Today, we do not have the gold standard. You may be thinking why did we need it in the first place? Well, in the past, it was always about trust and trade. If, let us say, country A is going to trade with country B, country A would say, "We will give you goods if you pay us in gold. We do not want your currency notes because your pieces of paper can just be printed."

This went on till 1914, the outbreak of World War One. When global peace was restored, countries stabilized their exchange rates and recreated the gold standard till 1929. What is so special about that year? Well, we had the Great Depression. When countries enter into a recession, they need to loosen monetary policy, meaning they have to increase money supply (print more money) to reduce interest rates. However, this was against the rule of the gold standard because countries could only print a certain amount of currency based on the amount of gold they had. They did not have the discretion to print more money than already allowed. So, during that time, because the countries were not able to respond, the recession worsened and turned into the Great Depression. The pain went on for a while until Japan decided to leave the gold standard. They decided that the interest of their country comes first and in that spirit printed a lot of Yen in order to lower the interest rates. Not surprisingly, Japan turned out to be the first country to recover from the Great Depression. Soon, other countries followed and eventually the gold standard was gone.

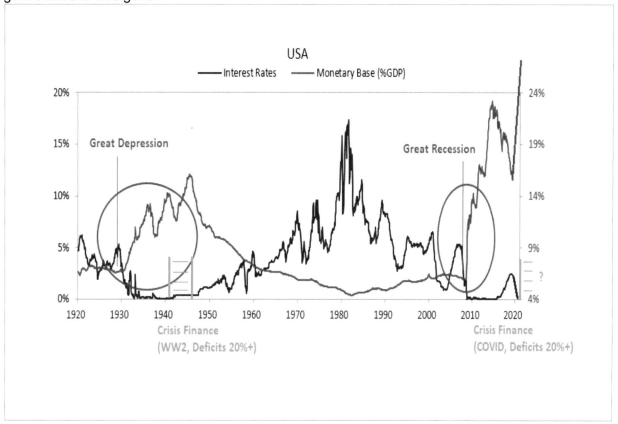

Source: https://twitter.com/LynAldenContact/status/1265428373255454721/photo/1

If you look at the chart above, you will see that in 1929, the blue line representing the interest rates actually went up. This was because people were desperate to borrow money, willing to pay whatever interest rate was out there in order to stay afloat. However, the Federal Reserve could not lower the interest rate because of the gold standard so the interest rate shot up and the country into the Great Depression and made things a lot worse. Next, look at the red line, representing the monetary base as a percentage of GDP, right below the blue line. You see a flat line due to the limited amount of gold that constrained the ability to print more US dollars. That is why the monetary base, or the money supply did not grow at all until the US decided to leave the gold standard. After that, the monetary base shot up and only came down during the

1960s. It was only due to that change in policy that the United States was finally able to escape the Great Depression.

The moment the US and other countries decided to leave the gold standard was the beginning of central banks making their own decisions regarding the creation of money supply every year. This is the heart of monetary policy.

Pros and Cons of the Gold Standard

The gold standard limited the amount of currency a country could print depending on how much gold they had. That meant that if a country wanted to be very successful in trade, they had to sell more goods in order to earn more US dollars which gave them the added flexibility to print more of their currency. The strength of the system was that it gave credibility to the currency that was printed. The weakness was that it cut off any idea of monetary policy whereby the country could not freely print any amount of currency it wished. In the aftermath of the Great Depression, the gold standard was abandoned and now, we have the US dollar as the reserve currency.

The Bretton Woods System and Agreement

In 1944, towards the end of World War II, the United States hosted a meeting for delegates from 44 countries at the United Nations Monetary and Financial Conference in Bretton Woods, New Hampshire. This was an important event because after the gold standard was abandoned, there were no rules governing how each country could print their currency. This led to great fluctuations in foreign exchange rates which hurt global trades. Non-US exporters and importers would not really know how much local currency they would have to pay or receive on an invoice, so, the US dollar could move up or down significantly. So, at the Bretton-Woods meeting, the countries came out with a new fixed exchange rate system anchored by the US dollar which in turn was connected to the gold standard.

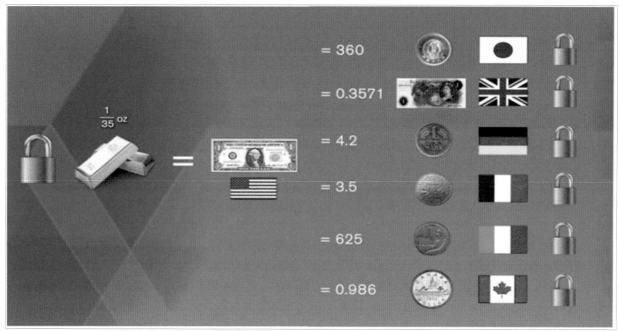

Source: Bloomberg

The Bretton Woods arrangement agreed on fixing 1/35th of an ounce to $1, or $35 to one ounce of gold. In turn, that $1 is locked in with ¥360, with £.3571, with DM 4.2, and so on. The world had a new arrangement where countries managed their own money supply to maintain the foreign exchange rate to ± 1% of the agreed lock, such as ¥360 to $1.

When Lyndon B. Johnson became president after the Kennedy assassination, he implemented the Great Society Programs which included Medicare (1965) and Medicaid (1965) that we all know today. There were other initiatives like the Water Quality Act and the Highway Act in the same time period.

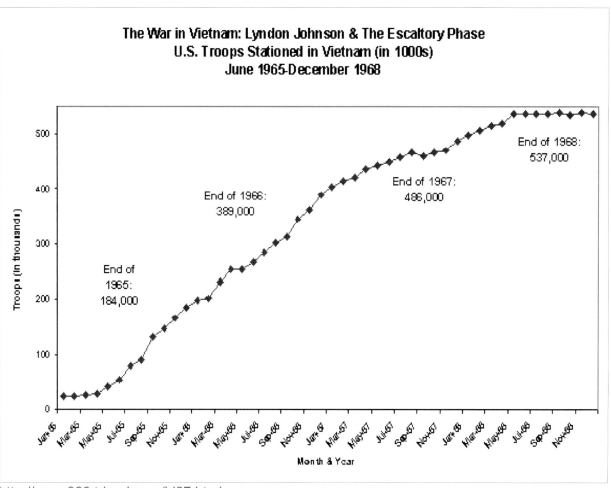

The War in Vietnam: Lyndon Johnson & The Escaltory Phase
U.S. Troops Stationed in Vietnam (in 1000s)
June 1965-December 1968

Along with these programs, the US was also involved in the Vietnam War and as you can see in the chart above, the number of troops that were stationed in Vietnam escalated. All this cost a great deal of money on top of the misery of war. In fact, things were so bad that economists came out with the Misery index, in which one would add up the rising inflation rate and the rising unemployment rate. When you added them both, the US was not in a good place at the time. All this happened at a time under the Bretton-Woods system, where the dollar was locked to gold. Other countries were alarmed to see the economic fundamentals and fiscal policies getting worse in the US. As more and more US dollars were being printed to pay for the fiscal initiatives and the Vietnam War, other countries decided to exchange their dollar reserve for gold.

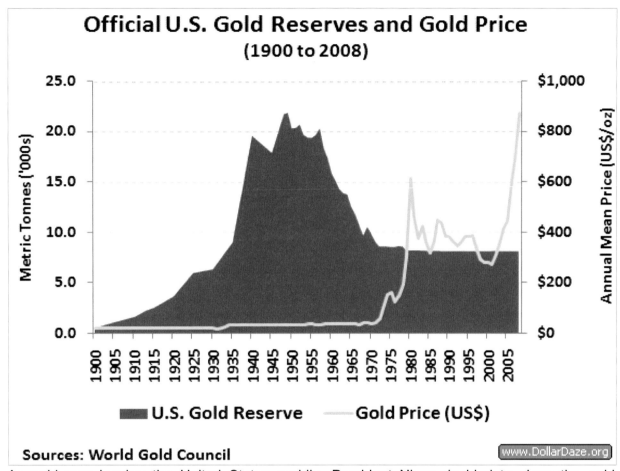

Official U.S. Gold Reserves and Gold Price
(1900 to 2008)

Metric Tonnes ('000s) — left axis: 25.0, 20.0, 15.0, 10.0, 5.0, 0.0

Annual Mean Price (US$/oz) — right axis: $1,000, $800, $600, $400, $200, $0

Years: 1900, 1905, 1910, 1915, 1920, 1925, 1930, 1935, 1940, 1945, 1950, 1955, 1960, 1965, 1970, 1975, 1980, 1985, 1990, 1995, 2000, 2005

Legend: ■ U.S. Gold Reserve   — Gold Price (US$)

Sources: World Gold Council

www.DollarDaze.org

As gold was leaving the United States rapidly, President Nixon decided to close the gold window on August 15, 1971 which marked the end of the Bretton Woods system of fixed exchange rates. The dollar went into a free fall and the price of gold shot up. Why would anyone hold the US dollar when it could no longer be convertible to gold?

A partial answer came when the United States and Saudi Arabia agreed that all oil transactions would be done in US dollars. This promoted the role of the US dollars as the reserve currency beyond the end of Bretton-Woods system. This is key because if you hold Singapore Dollars or most other currencies, you cannot use them to buy oil from Saudi Arabia. You will need to convert these currencies to US dollar to pay for the oil. Since the oil market is the largest commodity market, the decision to price oil in dollars rippled across many other commodities such as gold, iron, and copper, and very quickly most global trades followed suit and began to be invoiced in US dollar term.

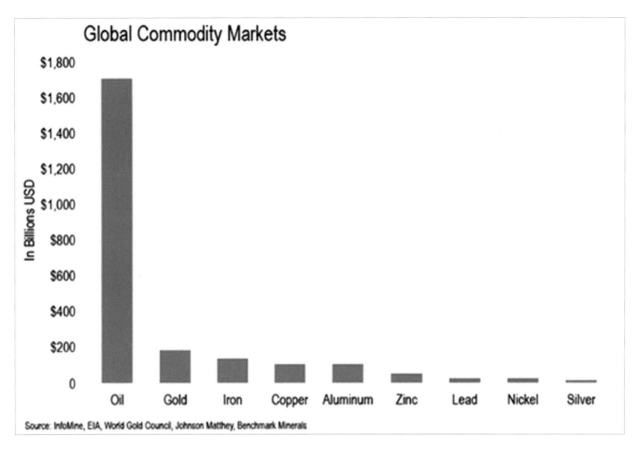

However, the world has changed quietly. The chart below shows that the US oil imports had declined gradually, over-shadowed by Chinese imports. China joined the World Trade Organization (WTO) and became a major manufacturer in the world which meant they needed a lot of oil. By 2017, China had surpassed the United States as the world's largest oil importer. In the United States, shale oil production became profitable and led to fewer oil imports. The United States became the world's largest oil producer in 2018.

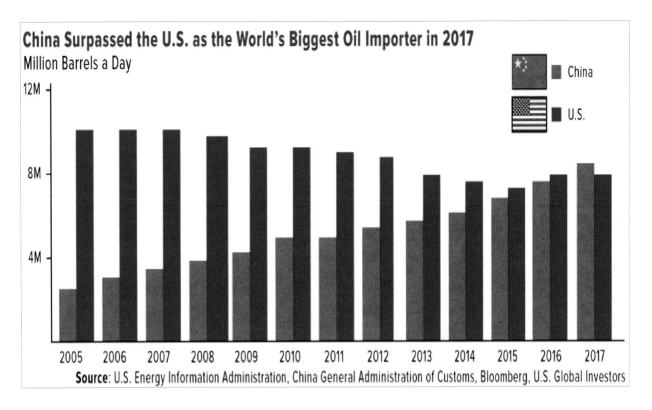

China Surpassed the U.S. as the World's Biggest Oil Importer in 2017

Million Barrels a Day

China
U.S.

Source: U.S. Energy Information Administration, China General Administration of Customs, Bloomberg, U.S. Global Investors

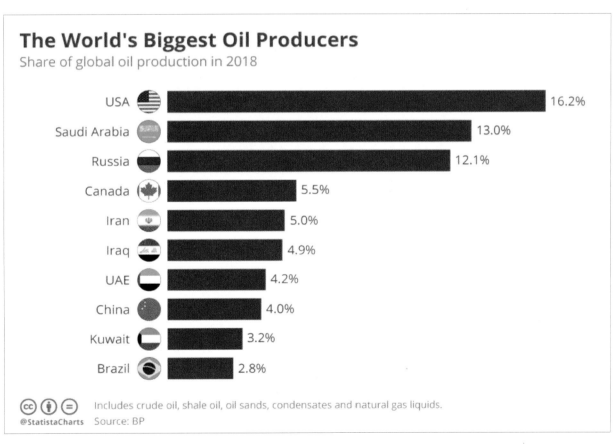

The World's Biggest Oil Producers

Share of global oil production in 2018

Country	Share
USA	16.2%
Saudi Arabia	13.0%
Russia	12.1%
Canada	5.5%
Iran	5.0%
Iraq	4.9%
UAE	4.2%
China	4.0%
Kuwait	3.2%
Brazil	2.8%

Includes crude oil, shale oil, oil sands, condensates and natural gas liquids.

@StatistaCharts   Source: BP

On September 1st, 2017, there was an extremely important news which surprisingly did not get much attention. The headlines read: *China sees new world order with oil benchmark backed by gold.* It was a Yuan-dominated contract that would let exporters circumvent US dollars. China had started an oil market denominated in Yuan terms (Renminbi is the official name of the Chinese currency and Yuan is the unit of this currency). Let's go back to our question, why would you hold US dollars? Our answer was we could buy oil with it. However, now as we think along the lines of Renminbi internationalization, we have a different set of questions in front of us, for instance, why would you hold the Renminbi? The answer to that from September 1st 2017 is you can buy oil with it!

When we look at China's crude oil import, one question arises: how difficult is it for China to persuade her oil trading partners to convert their dollar dominated oil contracts to Renminbi?

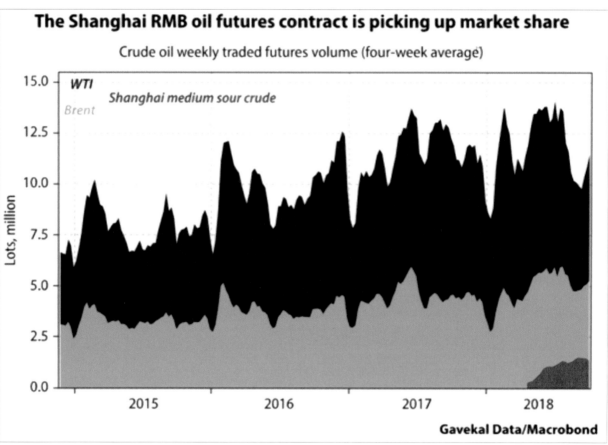

In the chart above, there is a small increase in Shanghai's medium sour crude, and when it grows over time, then the demand to US dollar for WTI and Brent oil would switch to demand for Renminbi to pay for oil.

The next chart shows how China is able to convince countries to denominate oil in Renminbi (CNY is also a symbol for Renminbi).

Nation	Net oil exports (000's b/d)	CNY Oil Supply/Pricing Deals
Saudi Arabia	7,016	Moving towards pricing oil in CNY
Russia	5,223	Pricing oil in CNY
Iraq	3,750	Building a refinery with Chinese companies, planning 3 more; profit-sharing/marketing-deal
Canada	2,897	Signed agreement to expand CNY trade usage in '14, named ICBC CNY-clearing bank in Canada
Iran	2,150	Pricing oil in CNY
UAE	2,065	Direct CNY/UAE Dirham trading (9/16); Dubai gold exchange launched CNY gold 4/17
Kuwait	2,025	China one of biggest drillers in Kuwait market with 45% market share of rigs
Angola	1,650	Made CNY 2nd currency in 2015
Nigeria	1,598	Nigeria, China Sign $2.4 Billion Currency-Swap to Lift Trade
Kazakhstan	1,424	Partially Chinese-owned, massive Kashagan oil field began shipping quarter 4/2016

Sources: Luke Gromen, FFTT, EIA, Incrementum AG

The chart below provides a snapshot of the international monetary system. In terms of foreign exchange markets, the US dollar accounts for about 60%, followed by the Euro at 20% and the Yen at less than 5%.

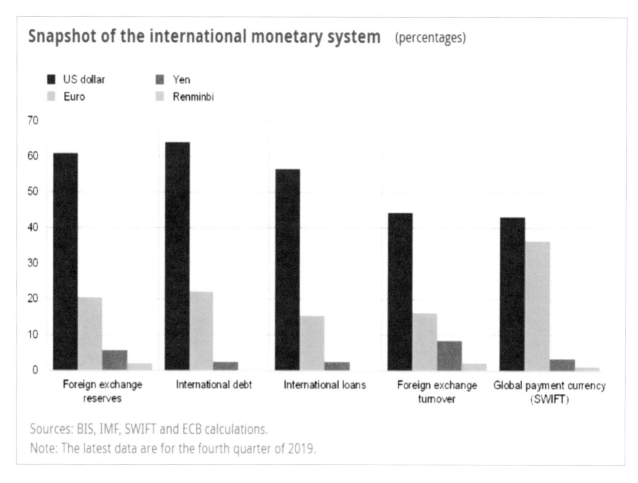

Snapshot of the international monetary system (percentages)

- ■ US dollar
- ■ Euro
- ■ Yen
- ■ Renminbi

Sources: BIS, IMF, SWIFT and ECB calculations.
Note: The latest data are for the fourth quarter of 2019.

In terms of foreign exchange turnover, the role of the Renminbi is not small. It is noteworthy that for global payment currency, the use of Euro is almost that of the US dollar. This is in large part due to fear that the US would weaponize the dollar by preventing a country or a foreign firm that has "unfriended" from accessing US dollars in the global payment system.

≡ Menu   Weekly edition   Q Search ⌄

Dethroning the dollar

Briefing

Jan 18th 2020 edition ›

America's aggressive use of sanctions endangers the dollar's reign

In 2018 America's Treasury put legal measures in place that prevented Rusal, a strategically important Russian aluminium firm, from freely accessing the dollar-based financial system—with devastating effect. Overnight it was unable to deal with many counterparties. Western clearing houses refused to settle its debt securities. The price of its bonds collapsed (the restrictions were later lifted). America now has over 30 active financial- and trade-sanctions

Although the dollar is still the reserve currency, we have to recognize whether it is shifting or not. As a watcher of currency markets, we have to be aware of such shifts over time. Meanwhile, a good question to ask is whether the world is a lot better since it abandoned the gold standard and switched to using the US dollar as the key reserve currency and if so, at what cost.

Triffin Dilemma

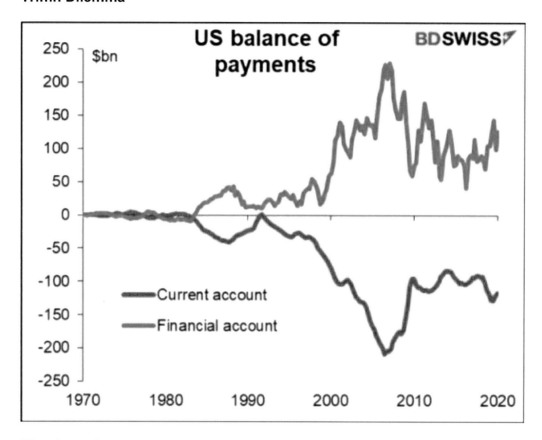

The chart above shows that the US has been running a current account deficit, mainly because it imports more than it exports. From this we know there is an excess supply of dollar to the world. What can the rest of the world can do with the "extra" US dollar? Why "extra"? If they would have bought the US exports, it would have been captured in the current account and the deficit would not be that large. Foreigners with these surplus US dollars are unlikely to leave them sitting idle in the banks. They would use the US dollars to buy US assets such as, equity, bonds, real estate, etc., which results in a capital account surplus; think of the US dollars coming home. The capital account also includes official reserve transactions account. To understand the reserve transactions, think of a group of Indonesian exporters who hold X number of US dollars but need to convert to Rupiah to pay their workers, suppliers etc. They would go to Bank Indonesia and sell US dollar in exchange for the local currency. Bank Indonesia would then invest the US dollars in US treasury bonds which would be accounted in the United States' official reserve transactions account. This example serves as a seed for the Triffin dilemma discussion.

The Triffin dilemma says that as global trades grow, the demand for US dollars will increase and will strengthen the US dollar which will then make US exporters less competitive, dragging down US GDP.
To meet this growing demand for US dollars, the United States will have to supply dollars to the world by running a current account deficit. Over time, as the current account gets larger and larger, it will undermine the status of the US dollar as a reserve currency. At some point in time, there will be less willingness to hold the currency of a country that is not export competitive and is "printing" more money via the current account deficit. In some ways, this scenario resembles the time when President Lyndon B. Johnson was running a serious budget deficit to fund the

Great Society programs and the Vietnam War, which eventually led to the breakdown of the gold standard and a sharp depreciation of the US dollar.

A more likely scenario is that before the large current account deficit becomes unacceptable by other countries, a domestic political problem will arise via a capital account surplus: the rest of the world will continue to recycle their trade surplus by buying up US assets in increasing amounts.

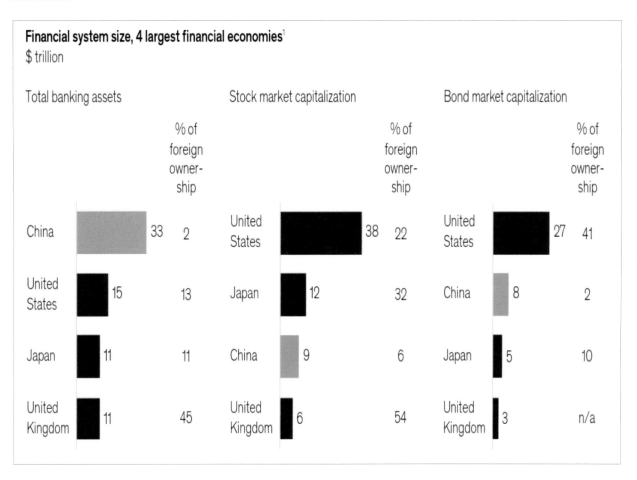

Financial system size, 4 largest financial economies[1]
$ trillion

Total banking assets		% of foreign owner-ship	Stock market capitalization		% of foreign owner-ship	Bond market capitalization		% of foreign owner-ship
China	33	2	United States	38	22	United States	27	41
United States	15	13	Japan	12	32	China	8	2
Japan	11	11	China	9	6	Japan	5	10
United Kingdom	11	45	United Kingdom	6	54	United Kingdom	3	n/a

Foreigners now own 13% of US banking assets, 22% of the stock market, and 41% of the bond market. If we look at the previous reserve currency country, UK, foreigners own 45% of its banking assets, 54% of their stock market, and 41% of their bond market.

Chapter 2 Trade Weighted Index and Dollar Cycle

Foreign Exchange Rate and the Trade Weighted Index

How do you tell if the US dollar is stronger or weaker? One way is to see how the US dollar trade against the Euro or the Yen. This is the common approach for a currency trader who will buy US dollar sell Euro/Yen if he thinks that the US dollar will weaken. However, if we want to see the full impact of dollar fluctuation, we have to recognize that the US trades with many countries. So, using a trade-weighted index (TWI) will be a more appropriate way to look at this impact. The index assigns the weights based on how important these countries are as trading partners for the US. Said another way: the Trade Weighted Dollar net out the US dollar strengthening and weakening against its major trading partners and weighs the various individual pairs of changes (US dollar against Yen, US dollar against Euro etc) according to trade volume. In a similar way, we can construct a Trade Weighted Yen or any other currency.

It is instructive to compare the TWI with the currencies in the chart below and to think about how the TWI movement can affect imported inflation and overall economic growth.

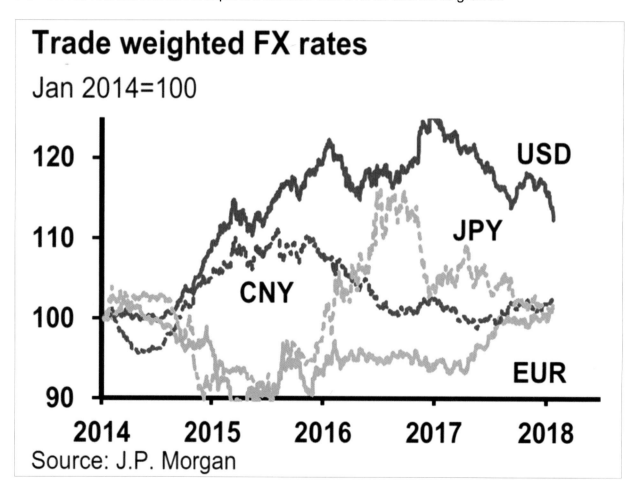

The chart below shows that the Dollar/Yen may move together in line with the Trade Weighted Yen but also at times, deviate from each other. In Q4, 2020, the Yen continued to strengthen against the US Dollar but weakened against its major trading partners with its TWI (Trade Weighted Index) falling from about 118 to about 116.

Trade-Weighted Index and REER

The chart below shows that although the Chinese currency, the Renminbi (RMB or CNY), is weakening against the US dollar, it is getting stronger in terms of real effective exchange rate. The exchange rate for CNY/USD, presented on the right axis, is getting larger in the last few years, which means that the Renminbi is weakening. In 2014 it cost only about 6 CNY to buy 1 USD but about 7 CNY in 2019/2020.

Real Effective Exchange Rate (REER) means that the exchange rate is trade weighted (TWI) and adjusted for inflation. We often see CPI used as the inflation indicator, but at times, unit labor cost is also common.

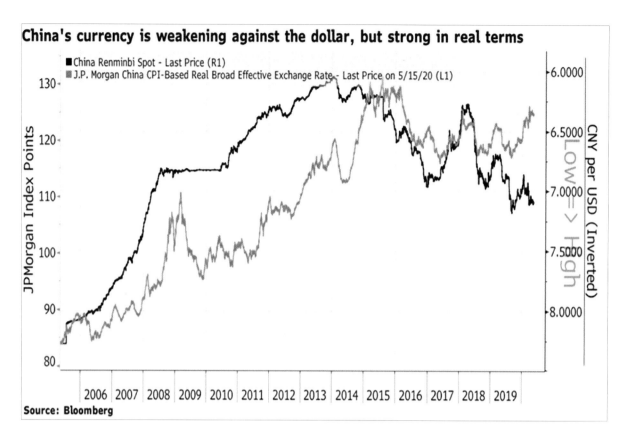

China's currency is weakening against the dollar, but strong in real terms

Source: Bloomberg

The key here is that there are two different ways of looking at a currency. If you are trading in the foreign exchange market, then you will watch the exchange rate between dollar and renminbi. However, if you are going to invest in the Chinese bond or equity market, then you are more interested in how the Chinese (real) trade-weighted currency index affects the Chinese economy.

Trade Weighted Dollar and US Import Prices

Intuitively, we know that a weaker US TWI will lead to an increase in US imports prices. The relationship between the two is shown below. A word of caution: what is not shown in the chart is that there is generally a 3-month lag. Still, you will notice, this is a lot clearer than just looking at USD/Yen or other pairs.

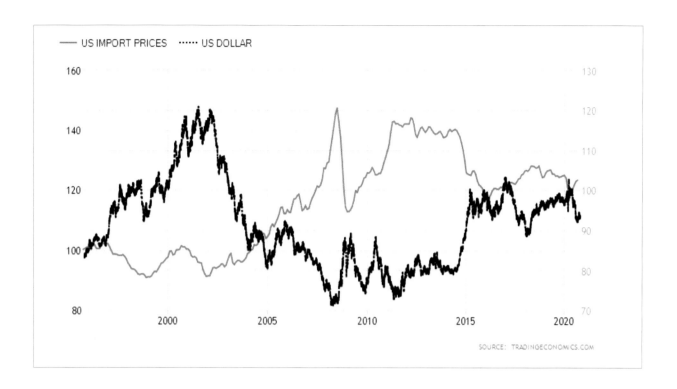

Trade Weighted Index and Exports

The chart below also confirms the intuitive reasoning that when the Chinese currency CNY weakens, that is good for Chinese exports. It shows that the correlation is very high and that there is a time lag.

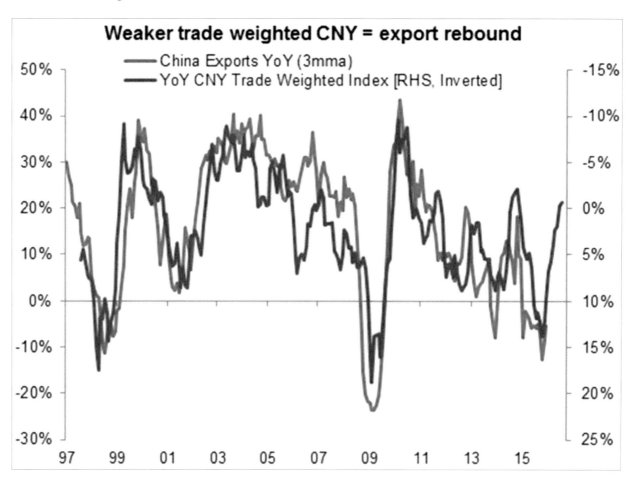

Source: @Callum_Thomas

Trade Weighted Index and World Trade

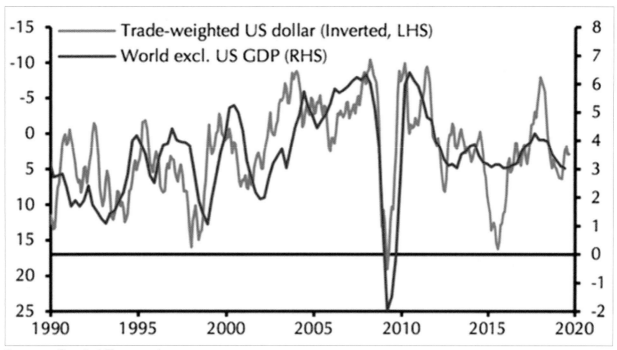

Source: Capital Economics

Instead of just looking at CNY and the Chinese exports, we can take a more global approach. The chart above shows that when the dollar strengthened, world's goods exports declined. Conversely, when the dollar weakens, the world's goods exports strengthen. Why does this happen? When we have a stronger US dollar, it equals to more Mexican Peso per $1 worth of import. So, goods are more expensive to the Mexicans and they naturally buy less. Recall that almost all commodities and global trades are invoiced in US dollar.

Could the Bank of Mexico intervene to prevent the Pesos from getting too weak They could sell US dollars and buy Pesos from the market. Two subsequent problems arise: first, by selling US dollars, at some point the central bank will "run out" of US dollar reserves. Second, when they buy Pesos from the market, Mexico's money supply would shrink, and their interest rates would go up which in turn would slow the economy down.

So, with or without the intervention from bank of Mexico, a stronger US TWI will weaken the Mexican economy. Multiply this framework for all the countries where imports are denominated in US dollar, you would see how world trade ex-US will weaken.

On the flip side, when the US TWI weakens, world trade ex-US will be stronger. Subsequently, this is also good for the stock markets, more so for Emerging Markets that relies more on global trade.

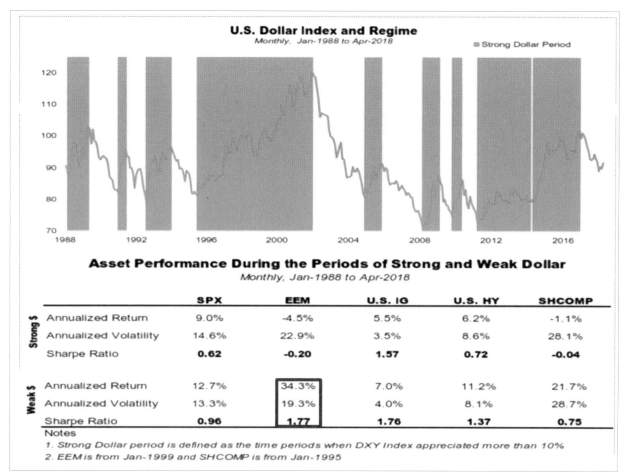

U.S. Dollar Index and Regime
Monthly, Jan-1988 to Apr-2018

■ Strong Dollar Period

Asset Performance During the Periods of Strong and Weak Dollar
Monthly, Jan-1988 to Apr-2018

		SPX	EEM	U.S. IG	U.S. HY	SHCOMP
Strong $	Annualized Return	9.0%	-4.5%	5.5%	6.2%	-1.1%
	Annualized Volatility	14.6%	22.9%	3.5%	8.6%	28.1%
	Sharpe Ratio	**0.62**	**-0.20**	**1.57**	**0.72**	**-0.04**
Weak $	Annualized Return	12.7%	34.3%	7.0%	11.2%	21.7%
	Annualized Volatility	13.3%	19.3%	4.0%	8.1%	28.7%
	Sharpe Ratio	**0.96**	**1.77**	**1.76**	**1.37**	**0.75**

Notes
1. Strong Dollar period is defined as the time periods when DXY Index appreciated more than 10%
2. EEM is from Jan-1999 and SHCOMP is from Jan-1995

Source: Gavekal

Pros and Cons of the US dollar as the reserve currency.

It is clear by now that the US dollar has an enormous influence on global trade as they are largely invoiced in US dollar. To understand the reach of the Dollar, the magic number is two-thirds:

- Two-thirds of global securities issuance and official foreign exchange (FX) reserves are denominated in US dollars.
- Two-thirds of Emerging Market (EM) external debt is denominated in US dollars. This means, for instance, when a Thai company wants to raise money in the global market, it will borrow the dollars from an American bank or issue US dollar denominated corporate bonds.
- The dollar serves as the monetary anchor in countries accounting for two-thirds of global GDP. The currency and monetary policies of countries like Singapore and Saudi Arabia follow the US interest rate policy very closely. For example, if the US cuts interest rates, Singapore would also follow with similar cuts.

As a consequence, the global financial cycle is, in reality, a US interest rate and a US dollar cycle. In simplistic terms, if we watch what is happening to the TWI US dollar, we can have a rough idea where the global trade will be heading. Strong dollar, weak global trade. Weak dollar, strong global trade, Emerging Market stocks would likely outperform.

Chapter 3 Exchange Rate Determinants

When I used to teach Econometrics, I saw students often spent too much time trying to get the best R-squared, the best t-value etc. and not enough time to understand how the different factors may or may not influence the dependent variables and why. Realistically, we cannot be sure if the model captures the right variables. If the selected variables are correct, then are the coefficients stable? We may never know about their true stability. It is important to bear in mind that coefficient or their importance changes overtime. Certain things which were important 3 years ago may not be so important today. The currency markets used to react dramatically to small changes in money supply and trade deficit data before shifting their key focus to Purchasing Managers Index (PMI) and employment data. For a few months in 2020, these were temporarily sidelined as investors pore over the number of people newly infected with COVID19. Following are some key exchange rate determinants that are always relevant:

1. **Relative Economic Growth Rate**

   Let's say we have country A and country B. Country A is growing faster than B and so, has a higher national income. The firms in Country A's company have higher profitability and its stock markets would likely be higher, at things being the same. There is a greater chance that the wages are also higher: if people in country A earn more, they will spend and invest more, which in turn will make the companies more profitable. These companies will then hire more employees. Overall, this country will have a positive growth cycle.

   When the country's economy is growing stronger and as global investors look for a better investment opportunity, it will attract foreign capital away from weaker economies. As capital flows to A from B, global investors will buy currency A and sell currency B. Hence, a stronger economy will lead to a stronger currency.

   To gauge relative economic growth, we can use the manufacturing PMI. The chart below shows that the Euro Area minus the US manufacturing PMI leads the Eur/USD by 3 months. The circled area suggests that the Euro will weaken against the USD soon.

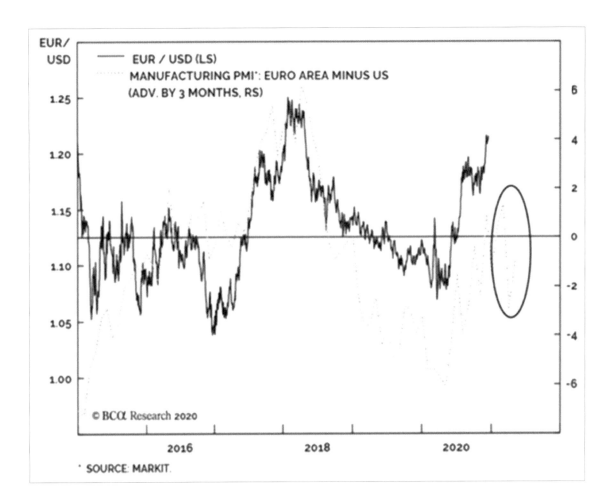

EUR/
USD

1.25

1.20

1.15

1.10

1.05

1.00

EUR / USD (LS)
MANUFACTURING PMI*: EURO AREA MINUS US
(ADV. BY 3 MONTHS, RS)

6

4

2

0

-2

-4

-6

© BCA Research 2020

2016   2018   2020

* SOURCE: MARKIT.

2. A) Commodity Exporting Countries

If you are asked to forecast a particular country's currency and that country is a commodity exporting country, then your work is a lot easier. Let us illustrate with an example. Using Federal Reserve Economic Database (FRED), we can compare oil prices and a country's exchange rate to make our forecast.

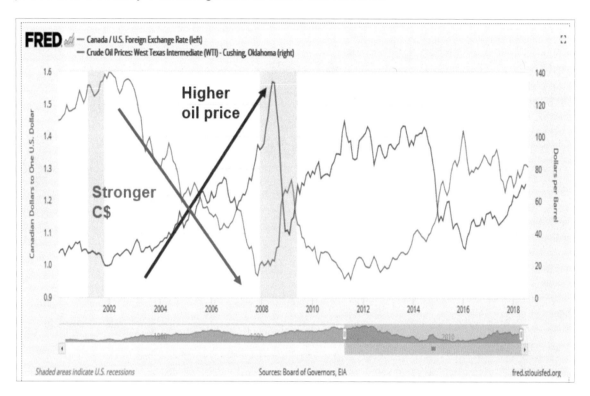

In the chart above, the red line is crude oil prices using the West Texas Instruments (WTI) and the blue line is the exchange rate between the Canadian and the US dollar. As you can see, higher oil prices correlate very well with a stronger Canadian dollar. Why would this be the case? When we have a higher oil price, with the same volume of oil being traded, the Canadian oil producers will have more US dollars to sell. More supply of US dollar in market would weaken it. At the same time, the Canadian producers would sell the US dollars to buy their local currency, which would strengthen the *loonie* (a nickname for the Canadian dollar named after the bird).

On the flip side, India is one of the world's largest oil importing countries. What is the impact of higher oil price on the Indian Rupee? Assume an annual import of 5 million barrels and oil prices jumped from $40 to $60 per barrel. Instead of USD200 m, India would have to buy USD 300 m to pay for the same amount of oil and sell a correspondingly larger amount of Rupee. Hence a weaker Rupee against the dollar, all things being equal. Realistically, the net effect on the exchange rate depends on how large this oil import is relative to other imports and to India's export, foreign direct investment, and other capital flows.

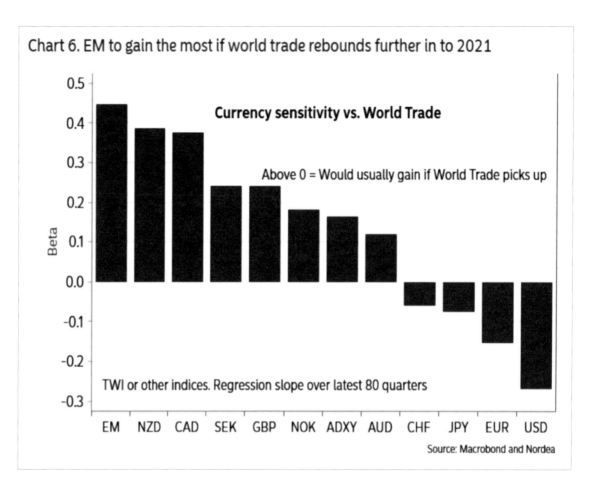

Chart 6. EM to gain the most if world trade rebounds further in to 2021

Currency sensitivity vs. World Trade

Above 0 = Would usually gain if World Trade picks up

TWI or other indices. Regression slope over latest 80 quarters

Source: Macrobond and Nordea

If we were to broaden the discussion beyond commodity exports and think in broader terms, we can appreciate how Emerging Markets (EM) currencies gain more when world trade improves since their exports and imports tend to have a larger share of their GDP. Along a spectrum, currencies like the New Zealand Dollar and the Canadian Dollar are more sensitive to global growth than the British Pound or the Norwegian Krone.

It is noteworthy that the US Dollar, Euro and Yen are negatively correlated to global trade. When global trade increases, their currencies weaken. This is easier to explain via the flip side: when global trade declines, there is often a high level of uncertainly in the world and as such, capital goes home to the US, Europe and Japan; investors sell other currencies and buy back their own US Dollars, Euro and Yen.

B) Trade and Current Account Deficit

US Trade Deficit and the US Dollar

trade balance $ billion per month, dollar exchange rate index

Trade deficit =
More imports than exports
= more supply of USD

Dollar depreciating

Federal Reserve, Nominal Trade Weighted Exchange Index Broad
Trade Balance, Total, Goods and services, SA

Source: Reuters EcoWin

In the chart above, we see the US trade deficit (Trade deficit imports are larger than exports). When US imports more than it exports, then they have to net pay to the rest of the world. This means there will be more US dollars circulating in the world. All things being equal, this would lead to a weaker dollar. Do note that when we look at the dollar index or any currency's trade-weighted index, the smaller that number, the weaker its trade weighted.

The trade balance is important because it is often the largest component of the current account balance. The chart below explores how current account relates to currency performance. Anything on the right of 0 on the horizontal axis depicts a current account surplus. Conversely, on the left of it is a current account deficit. The vertical axis is the currency compared to the dollar a year ago. On that particular day, the correlation stood out very clearly: when these countries had a current account deficit, their currencies had been weaker against the US dollar, meaning these countries have to net pay for the good and services they received net of what they can offer vis a vis the rest of the world.

On the flip side, large current account surpluses were not correlated with a stronger currency. One possible reason is that these countries had intervened in the currency markets to prevent their own currencies from getting too strong and hurting their exporters' competitive advantage. On the other hand, countries with current account deficit were unable to support their weakening currencies; requiring them to buy back their own currencies and selling their US dollar reserves which are likely to be limited.

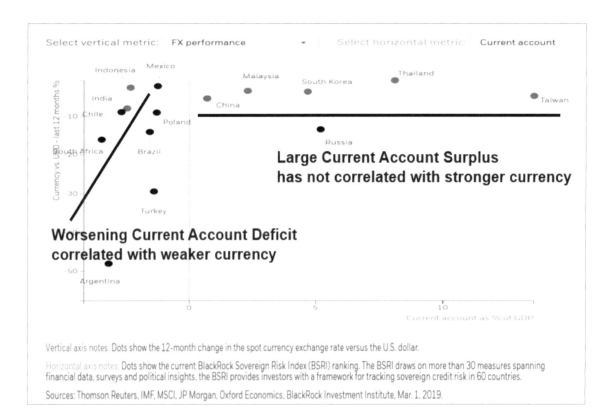

Select vertical metric: FX performance ▾   Select horizontal metric: Current account

Large Current Account Surplus has not correlated with stronger currency

Worsening Current Account Deficit correlated with weaker currency

Vertical axis notes: Dots show the 12-month change in the spot currency exchange rate versus the U.S. dollar.

Horizontal axis notes: Dots show the current BlackRock Sovereign Risk Index (BSRI) ranking. The BSRI draws on more than 30 measures spanning financial data, surveys and political insights, the BSRI provides investors with a framework for tracking sovereign credit risk in 60 countries.

Sources: Thomson Reuters, IMF, MSCI, JP Morgan, Oxford Economics, BlackRock Investment Institute, Mar. 1, 2019.

C) Fiscal Deficit

When a country like the US runs a wide budget deficit, it is spending more than the taxes it collects. Often at a time when the country is in a recession this shortfall means it will have to issue more bonds. In the chart below, the fiscal deficit is depicted by the red line and if we follow it, we see a brief period of fiscal surplus between 2000 and 2004. After that, there has been greater fiscal deficit. You will also see that it has a nice correlation to the trade-weight dollar index. In 2020, the market expected the budget deficit to worsen significantly because of a sharp increase in stimulus spending to support the economy during the COVID19 crisis. If the correlation is similar to the past, then it is likely that the trade-weighted dollar will decline significantly.

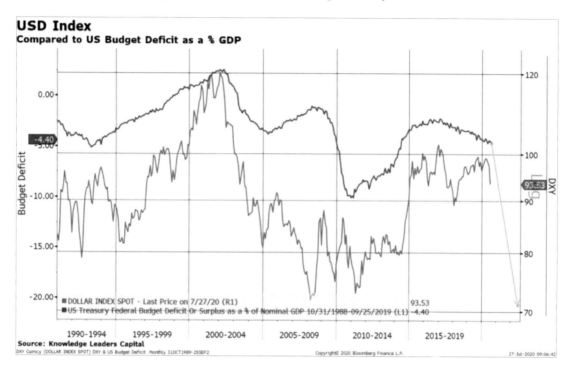

D) Twin Deficit

The fiscal and current account deficit when combined together is often referred to as the twin deficit. It is similar to the misery index, where we also add two unhappy numbers: the unemployment and inflation rates. The twin deficit shows how bad a shape the country is in. The chart below shows the US twin deficit as a percentage of GDP advancing 18 months, represented by the red line. It has a very clear relationship with the US nominal effective exchange rate, represented by the black line.

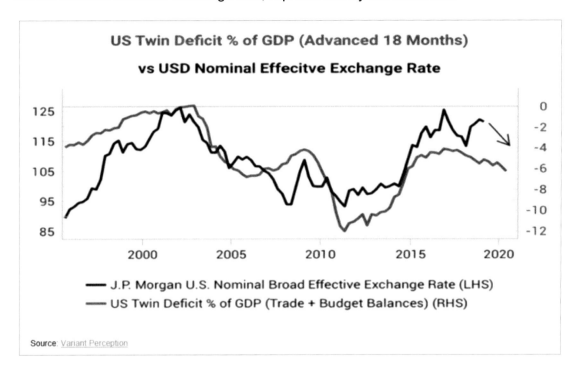

US Twin Deficit % of GDP (Advanced 18 Months)

vs USD Nominal Effecitve Exchange Rate

— J.P. Morgan U.S. Nominal Broad Effective Exchange Rate (LHS)
— US Twin Deficit % of GDP (Trade + Budget Balances) (RHS)

Source: Variant Perception

3. **A) Interest Rate Theoretical Framework**

    - **The Fisher Effect**

      It begins by assuming real interest rates are same in every country. The country with the highest interest rate should have a higher inflation. This leads to the International Fisher Effect (IFE) which says that the currency of country with the lower interest rate will strengthen in the future. However, as a practitioner, I have trouble accepting the Fisher Effect's assumption as real interest rates cannot be same in every country (It is as silly as assuming every person is of the same height). If you were to draw a chart in any particular time period, you will find that the real interest rates, whether it is 10Y or 5Y, are all over the place and are rarely, if ever, the same.

    B) Nominal Interest Rate Differential

    Let's examine the newspaper headline below. If the Reserve Bank of New Zealand were to reduce interest rates, the Kiwi (New Zealand Dollar) could drop sharply. This could be because of the interest rate differential: Partly due to the foreign money which had been invested in New Zealand for the previously high interest rates returning home to Japan, Europe or the United States. And partly on fears that if the central bank is easing monetary policy, it is likely confirming that the economy is slowing and consequently, there will be less investment opportunities in the country.

    ## New Zealand Dollar Sinks as RBNZ Deputy Governor Hints at Rate Cut

    Feb 21, 2019 10:30 pm -05:00
    by Ilya Spivak , *Sr. Currency Strategist*

    NEW ZEALAND DOLLAR, RBNZ - TALKING POINTS:

    - *New Zealand Dollar down after RBNZ's Bascand hints at a rate cut*
    - *Easing may be needed as new bank capital rules boost lending costs*
    - *Priced-in 2019 market view puts chance of easing at 20-30 percent*

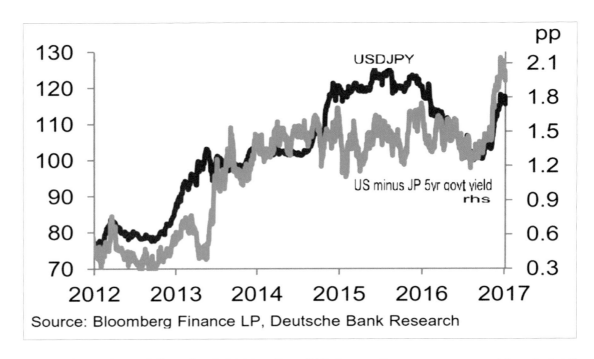

Source: Bloomberg Finance LP, Deutsche Bank Research

In the chart above follow the light blue line (US-Japan 5-year government bond yield) on the right-hand side. The spread between the US and Japan widened approximately from 0.3% to 2.1%. During that period, when the US interest rate was much higher than that of the Yen, money flowed out of Japan into the US. That's why the US dollar strengthened against the Yen from about 80 to 130 yen. This is often called a carry trade.

C) Inflation Rate Differential

The chart below shows foreign exchange rate changes of various countries with respect to their inflation rates (denoted by the Consumer Price Index - CPI). For instance, Turkey has a very high inflation and correspondingly a very weak Turkish Lira against the US dollar. On the other end, countries like China, Indonesia and Chile which have a lower inflation have relatively less currency weakness.

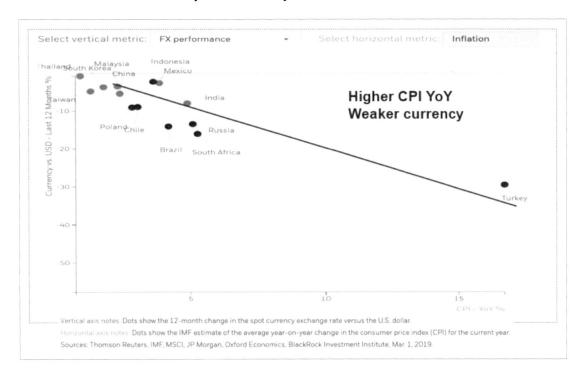

D) Purchasing Power Parity (PPP)

Related to interest rate inflation, we have the Purchasing Power Parity (PPP). The PPP essentially argues that the prices of goods in country A and B should be the same over time. The key factor is the exchange rate. If you can value the two goods in A and B, then you can count whether the currency is under or over-valued. If a Big Mac costs $5.80 in Singapore dollar in Singapore and $5.74 in US dollar in the United States. The implied exchange rate would be 1.01 (5.80/5.74). This rate can also be regarded as the "fair value". The difference between the "fair value" and the actual exchange rate, which was 1.36 at that time, suggests that the Singapore dollar was 25.8% under-valued. So, we should expect the Singapore dollar to strengthen overtime from 1.36 to 1.01.

One could argue that just comparing the cost of goods of two different countries using a hamburger is silly and too narrow. Hence, investors apply the PPP by using a basket of comparable goods and services. The CPI which tracks the spending by the average household in each country serves this purpose very well by tracking relative inflation between pairs of countries.

In the two charts below, you can see that the market exchange rates for the USD-RMB and USD-Euro tracks the PPP value closely over a few years. This model cannot be applied to weekly or daily movement.

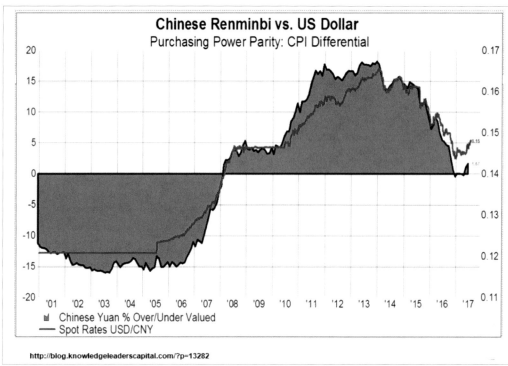

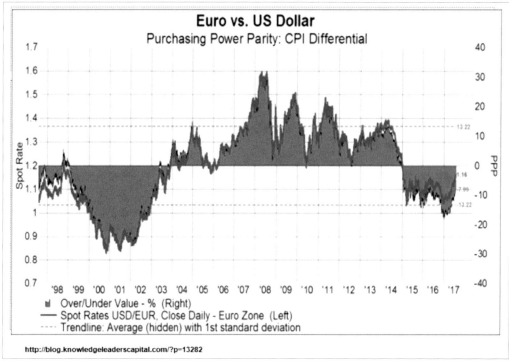

E) My Framework on Interest Rate

A lot depends on the reason for the higher interest rate. For example, when Japan has a lower interest rate than the US, money would flock to the US. We need to fine tune this thinking because realistically, the Japanese are unlikely to move money into Turkey where the interest rate is a lot higher. So, we need to break down the higher interest rates into two components. If the interest rate is driven by higher inflation, then countries like Turkey is not in a happy place; no capital would flow in. Rather, it is likely that capital may flow out and its currency will weaken. Conversely, if it is driven by higher real rates, say Australia, then it would suggest the economy is strongly growing, creating greater investment opportunities. This optimism will draw in capital from abroad and the Australian dollar will strengthen.

It would also depend on the stage of the monetary policy tightening stage. If it is early stage, then it has a positive effect. Conversely, if it is in a late stage, then it has a negative effect. When the economy recovers from a recession and starts to power up, the Fed will need to raise rates from being (very) stimulative back to neutral. We will begin a time period where companies will start to revise their earnings upward. The Fed may raise the rate between .25-.75% and it would not matter that much as this amount of rate hike is very small in the initial stage compared to the company's upward revision of earnings. However, at the tail end of tightening, when the Fed had raised interest rate by, say 2.5-3%, the cumulative increase in interest rates begins to bite and slow down the economy. Around the time when the economy no longer shows broad based growth, that is when the analysts start to revise down company's earning and profitability. And as global investors start to expect a recession to occur soon, money will flow out of the US and the US dollar weakens, all things being the same.

4. Money Supply

After the COVID19 crisis, the market fixated on relative money supply among countries. If the chart below tracks the Olympic type of gamesmanship, the United States wins the gold medal for creating the highest amount of new currency in the system as measured by the 438% increase in M2 annual growth rate in 2020 compared to a year ago. The United Kingdom comes in with a weak silver medal of "only" 237%. All things being equal and thinking in simple supply and demand terms, when more US dollars are created and supplied to the world than the Euro and the Yen, it should weaken.

Growth of US monetary aggregates outpaces all others			
	M2 annual growth (%) 2019	M2 annual growth (%) 2020	Increase in the rate of change (%)
United States	4.33	23.3	438
Eurozone	5.5	8.5	55
Japan	2.6	5.1	96
China	8.5	11.1	31
United Kingdom	2.7	9.1	237
Switzerland	3.6	0.8	-78

Source: Gavekal

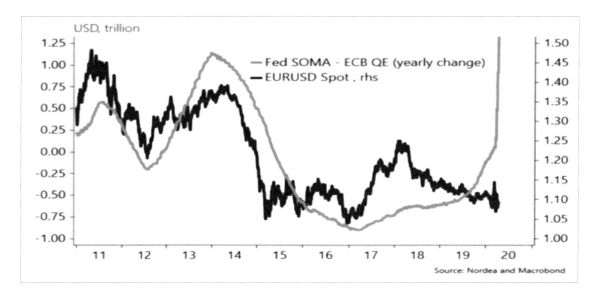

When we look at the relative comparison in the chart above, you will see a positive relationship. SOMA stands for System Open Market Account and it tracks the amount of new money created, mainly from the Quantitative Easing operations. So, the spike up in FED QE minus the ECB QE can lead one to conclude that more new US dollars relative to new Euro will lead to a weaker dollar against the Euro

5. Capital Flow

Capital flow is significantly more important as a determinant of exchange rate for Emerging Markets (EM) than for the US. In EMs, the stock and bond market are very small compared to that of the United States. $1 billion coming out of the US has a lot less impact on the US but could greatly affect these EMs, especially in the foreign exchange markets.

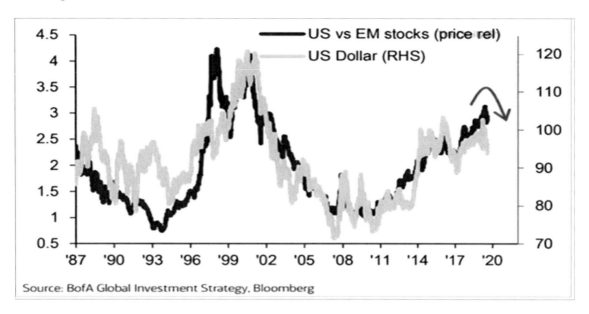

Source: BofA Global Investment Strategy, Bloomberg

When you look at the chart above, it expands on the market expecting the dollar to weaken. To the extend we expect the US dollar to weaken and if the historical relationship is the same, then we can expect the US stock market to underperform the EMs. When more capital flows into the EMs, they benefit from a positive cycle of stronger stock market, stronger currencies, and less inflation.

Unlike Foreign Direct Investments, the sort of capital that moves into stock and bonds is often referred to as 'hot money'. Astute investors watch how the countries receiving these hot money are prepared for the day when a set of bad news could lead to a sudden outflow of all the accumulated inflow. The greater the sum of these money, the greater the risk of the outflow and the more painful it will be when they leave.

6. Speculation

A) Technical Analysis

In the foreign exchange market, it is common to use technical analysis. If one were to see the chart below as a self-fulfilling prophecy, one can see how the uptrend line provided a visual signal to buy when it touches the uptrend line AND sell if it breaks, IF enough people believe it. An analogy is the traffic light: it works only when people agree or believes that we should stop at red and go at green.

However, unlike the traffic light, technical analysis also has the rubber band effect; it does not work if too many people had bought or had sold and pushed prices to the extreme.

The chart below shows that when prices are too far away from its simple moving average (could be 50 days or 200 days), prices will reverse and move back towards the mean.

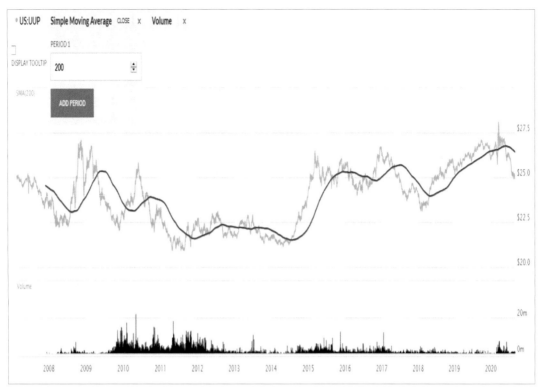

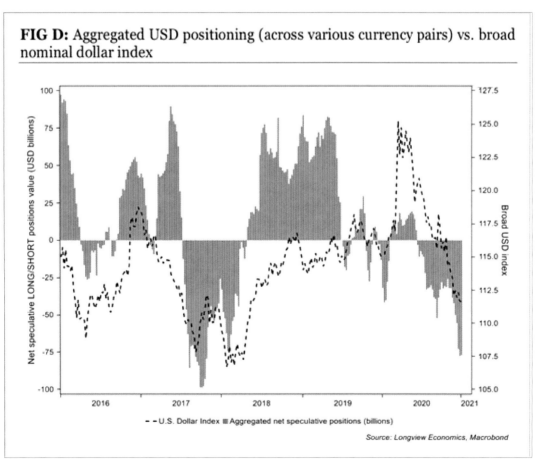

FIG D: Aggregated USD positioning (across various currency pairs) vs. broad nominal dollar index

- - U.S. Dollar Index   ▦ Aggregated net speculative positions (billions)

Source: Longview Economics, Macrobond

The likelihood of a correction increases when too many market participants are on the same side of the market. This reflects the saying 'the market will do whatever it takes to hurt the greatest number of people.'

The chart above shows when the aggregated net speculative positions are at the extreme, the trend reverses. In the early 2021, the Broad TWI US dollar is likely to correct and trade upwards as it did in 2017 when the market was also net very short the dollar. A small amount of good news would trigger a short squeeze.

B) Fundamental Analysis

One of the key fundamental drivers of an exchange rate is the relative growth rate with capital flows towards the country with stronger growth and more investment opportunities. What are the economic indicators that are followed very closely? The number one indicator for the United States is the Non-Farm Payroll. Agricultural jobs are excluded because a lot of the work is done by illegal immigrants and understandably such data is very difficult to collect. Hence, they are excluded. The second popular indicator is GDP followed by ISM non-manufacturing, average hourly earnings, ISM manufacturing, retail sales and the data from the payroll processing firm ADP* (Automated data processing), Chicago's purchasing manager's, housing starts and Existing Home Sales.

7. Central Bank Intervention – Plaza Accord

The most famous central bank intervention is the Plaza Accord. On September 21st, 1985, at the New York Plaza hotel, Treasury Secretary James Baker invited the finance ministers from major countries and told them that the US dollar was too strong and was hurting the US exports and should be weakened; the other countries were asked to strengthen their own currency. As you can see in the chart below, after this intervention the trade weighted US dollar weakened significantly.

---

* A lot of the companies have outsourced their payroll to ADP. So, a few days before the payroll day, the HR would email them and provide updates before they prepare the payroll, telling who has been fired, who has been hired at what salary, etc. ADP has all these data and publishes it.

Source: Board of Governors of the Federal Reserve System (US)
Shaded areas indicate US recessions - 2015 research.stlouisfed.org

When and why central banks intervene in the currency markets?

Central bank would always be concerned that if their currency is too strong, it would hurt their exporters. For instance, let us say, the Thai Baht is too strong, then the Thai exporters would complain about their lack of competitiveness in the market. For every one US dollar of sales, they would get fewer Thai Baht. If they wish to get the same amount of Thai Baht, they will have to raise the price in US dollar terms and risk losing sales. In either case, net exports will drag down the GDP growth. To mitigate this, the Bank of Thailand could weaken the Thai Baht by selling Baht and buying US dollar in the market. This can continue until the Bank of Thailand increases so much of its domestic currency that the money supply causes inflation.

What happens on the flip side when a country has a weak currency? Let us use a weak Indonesian Rupiah scenario. It is good news for the exporters. However, Bank Indonesia would be concerned with imported inflation. For the same amount of oil imported and same oil price, which is denominated in US dollar terms, it would now cost more Rupiah. Importers would likely have no choice but to pass on this cost increase to their Indonesian customers, hence, higher imported inflation.

Bank Indonesia would buy Rupiah, sell US dollar in the market. Most observers would argue that this sort of central bank intervention in the foreign exchange market is very likely to fail because the amount of US dollars the Bank Indonesia has is limited. Sooner or later, they would have no more dollars to sell.

However, learning from the 2008 crisis, the Federal Reserve has created a new weapon: liquidity swap. The Fed can just lend US dollars to Bank Indonesia. This crisis calming weapon or balm was in full display during the COVID19 crisis when the Fed successfully lent enough dollar to the key central banks to cool down a sudden surge in demand for US dollars, mainly because US investors were selling assets around the world and bringing money home. As you can see in chart below, almost $450 billion was lent out and quickly repaid over in just a 3-month period.

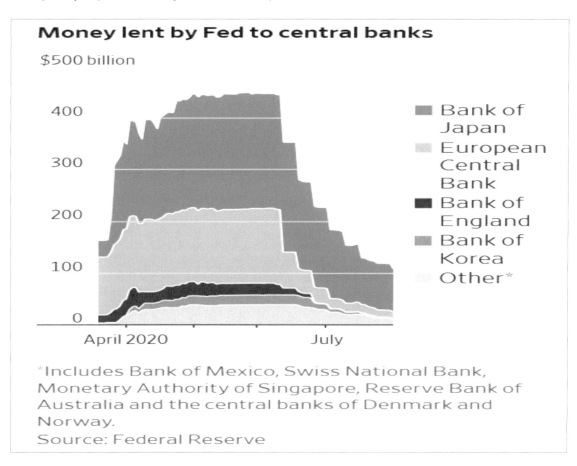

Money lent by Fed to central banks

$500 billion

*Includes Bank of Mexico, Swiss National Bank, Monetary Authority of Singapore, Reserve Bank of Australia and the central banks of Denmark and Norway.
Source: Federal Reserve

https://www.wsj.com/articles/fed-federal-reserve-jerome-powell-covid-coronavirus-dollar-lending-economy-foreign-currency-11596228151

Made in the USA
Middletown, DE
02 August 2023

36127145R00027